Matter and Energy

Principles of Matter and Thermodynamics

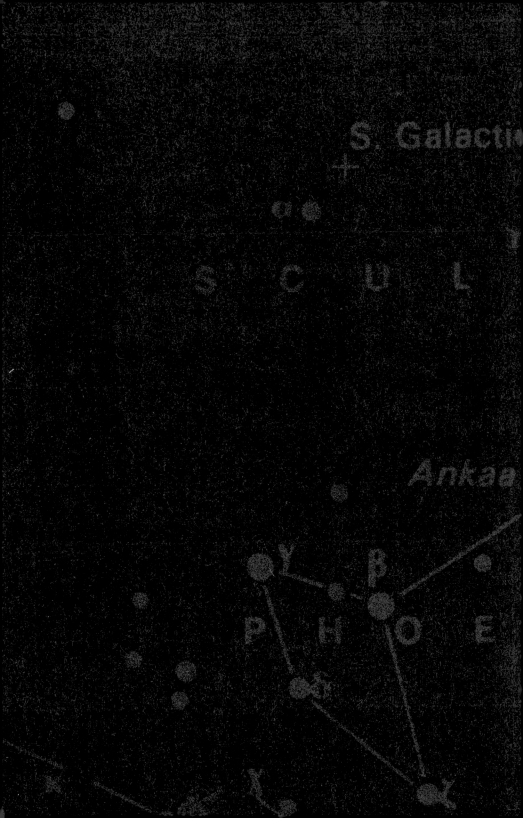

T112041

Matter and Energy

Principles of Matter and Thermodynamics

by Paul Fleisher

Lerner Publications Company · Minneapolis

This book is dedicated to my students, past, present, and future.

The text for this book has been adapted from a single-volume work entitled *Secrets of the Universe: Discovering the Universal Laws of Science,* by Paul Fleisher, originally published by Atheneum in 1987. Illustrations by Tim Seeley were commissioned by Lerner Publications Company. New back matter was developed by Lerner Publications Company.

Lerner Publications Company
A division of Lerner Publishing Group
241 First Avenue North
Minneapolis, Minnesota 55401 U.S.A.

Website address: www.lernerbooks.com

Library of Congress Cataloging-in-Publication Data

Fleisher, Paul
Matter and energy : principles of matter and thermodynamics /
    by Paul Fleisher
        p.   cm. — (Secrets of the universe)
    Includes bibliographical references and index.
    ISBN 0-8225-2986-6 (lib. bdg. : alk. paper)
    1. Matter—Constitution—Juvenile literature. 2. Thermodynamics—Juvenile
    literature. [1. Matter—Constitution. 2. Thermodynamics.] I. Title. II. Series.
    QC173.16 .F54 2002
    530.11–dc21   00-009836

Manufactured in the United States of America
2 3 4 5 6 7 – JR – 07 06 05 04 03 02

Contents

Introduction: What Is a Natural Law? 6

   1. The Law of Conservation of Matter 10

   2. How the Elements Combine 15
      The Law of Definite Proportions and
      Gay-Lussac's Law

   3. Mendeleyev's Periodic Law 23

   4. The First Law of Thermodynamics 34
      Conservation of Energy

   5. The Second Law of Thermodynamics . .42
      Entropy

Timeline 50

Biographies of Scientists 52

For Further Reading 58

Selected Bibliography 60

Glossary 61

Index 62

About the Author 64

INTRODUCTION

Everyone knows what a law is. It's a
rule that tells people what they must or
must not do. Laws tell us that we
shouldn't drive faster than the legal
speed limit, that we must not take
someone else's property, that we must
pay taxes on our income each year.

Where do these laws come from? In the United States
and other democratic countries, laws are created by elected
representatives. These men and women discuss ideas they
think would be fair and useful. Then they vote to decide
which ones will actually become laws.

But there is another kind of law, a scientific law. You
probably have heard about the law of conservation of
energy, for example. It says that energy—such as heat,
light, motion, or electricity—can neither be created nor
destroyed. Where did that law come from? Who made it,
and what could we do if we decided to change it?

The law of conservation of energy is very different from

a speed limit or a law that says you must pay your taxes. Speed limits are different in different places. On many interstate highways, drivers can travel 65 miles per hour. On crowded city streets, they must drive more slowly. But the law of conservation of energy works exactly the same way no matter where you are. In the country or the city, in France, Brazil, or the United States, you can't create energy out of nothing, or make it disappear either.

Sometimes people break laws. When speed limit signs say 55, people often drive 60 or even faster. But what happens when you try to break the law of conservation of energy? You can't. There are no magic words or special procedures you can use to make heat or light suddenly appear or to cause them to simply vanish.

The law of conservation of energy doesn't apply just to people, either. All things obey this law: plants, animals, water, stones, even planets and stars. And the law stays in effect whether people are watching or not.

The law of conservation of energy is a natural law, or a rule of nature. Scientists and philosophers have studied events in our world for a long time. They have made careful observations and done many experiments. And they have found that certain events happen over and over again in a regular, predictable way.

You have probably noticed some of the same things yourself. Conservation of energy is a good example. Heat and light don't just appear or disappear. You know that from your own experience. A magician might seem to light an electric bulb that isn't connected to any wires or other energy source. But we know it's a trick. What makes the trick interesting is that we know it's not really possible for him to have done it.

A scientific law is a statement that tells how things work in the universe. It describes the way things are, not the way we want them to be. That means a scientific law is not something that can be changed whenever we choose. We can change the speed limit or the tax rate if we think they're too high or too low. But no matter how much we want to make light magically appear or cause a distant object to move, conservation of energy remains in effect. We cannot change that fact; we can only describe what happens. A scientist's job is to describe the laws of nature as accurately and exactly as possible.

The laws you will read about in this book are universal laws. They are true not only here on earth, but also throughout the universe. The universe includes everything we know to exist: our planet, our solar system, our galaxy, all the other billions of stars and galaxies, and all the vast empty space in between. All the evidence that scientists have gathered about the other planets and stars in our universe tells us that scientific laws that apply here on earth also apply everywhere else.

In the history of science, some laws have been found through the brilliant discoveries of a single person. But ordinarily, scientific laws are discovered through the efforts of many scientists, each one building on what others have done earlier. When one scientist receives credit for discovering a law, it's important to remember that many other people also contributed to that discovery.

Scientific laws do change, on rare occasions, but they don't change because we tell the universe to behave differently. Scientific laws change only if we have new information or more accurate observations. The law changes when scientists make new discoveries that show the old law doesn't describe the universe as well as it should. Whenever scientists agree to a change in the laws of nature, the new law describes events more completely, or more simply and clearly.

The law of conservation of energy is a good example of this. In the early twentieth century, Albert Einstein realized that matter (or mass) can be transformed into energy. The energy doesn't just appear from nowhere. It is actually matter changed to a different form.

Einstein also discovered that high levels of energy can add to an object's mass. As an object accelerates toward the speed of light, gaining energy as it does, it becomes more and more massive. So modern science no longer identifies separate laws of conservation of energy and conservation of mass. Instead, there is one law—the law of conservation of mass-energy.

Natural laws are often written in the language of mathematics. This allows scientists to be more exact in their descriptions of how things work. For example, you've probably heard of Einstein's equation: $E = mc^2$.

It's one of the most famous equations in science. But don't let the math fool you. It's simply a mathematical way of saying that mass (m) can be changed into energy (E). Writing it this way lets scientists compute the amount of energy contained in a certain amount of matter.

The science of matter and energy, and how they behave, is called physics. In the hundreds of years that physicists have been studying our universe, they have discovered many natural laws. In this book, you'll read about several of these great discoveries. There will be some simple experiments you can do to see the laws in action. Read on, and share the fascinating stories of the laws that reveal the secrets of our universe.

CHAPTER 1

The Law of Conservation of Matter

Magicians love to make objects appear and disappear. Coins suddenly appear behind someone's ear, a rabbit pops out of an empty hat, or a beautiful woman vanishes into thin air. Almost every magician depends on mysterious appearances and disappearances for many tricks.

When we see a magician make something appear or disappear, we're fascinated. Why? We're amazed because we know that in real life objects don't appear from or vanish into thin air. We know that you can't turn something into nothing or nothing into something. Without realizing it, we're using the *law of conservation of matter*.

The law of conservation of matter is usually stated like this: Matter can neither be created nor destroyed. Matter, of course, is stuff. It is any kind of stuff—solid, liquid, or gas. The law of conservation of matter says that whatever anyone does to an object, the matter it is made of will continue to exist, in some form or another. This law is also known as the *law of conservation of mass*. Mass is the measurement of the amount of matter that any object contains.

A rock is a piece of matter. Let's use it as an example. Suppose we hit our rock with a sledgehammer and break it into pieces. Is the rock still there? Of course. It has just changed form.

Let's grind our pieces of rock into a fine powder and toss it up into the wind. The powder blows away. Have we destroyed anything? No. The same amount of rock still exists, but now it has become tiny particles scattered far and wide.

Perhaps some of our rock powder falls into a farmer's field. A corn plant absorbs some of the minerals through its roots. The rock becomes part of the corn plant, but it still exists. If we eat the corn, the minerals become part of our body. Still nothing has been destroyed.

Suppose we wanted to try these experiments, but we didn't have a rock. No matter where we looked, we just couldn't find a rock! Could we create one? Could we say some sort of magic spell that would make a rock appear from nowhere? Of course not. It seems very clear that matter cannot be created, either.

But grinding a rock into powder is just a physical change. No matter how fine we grind the rock, it's still rock. In chemical reactions, totally new substances are formed. For example, when we mix vinegar and baking soda, carbon dioxide gas is formed. The gas wasn't there before the reaction took place. Has new matter been created? Has any of the vinegar or baking soda been destroyed?

Fire is one type of chemical reaction. Think about what happens when you burn a piece of paper. You start out with a full-sized sheet of paper, but after the flames die out, all that's left is a little pile of ash. If you weigh the paper before and after you burn it, you'll discover that the paper weighs much more than the ashes that are left behind. It certainly looks as though matter is destroyed by fire. If you had been a scientist in the early 1700s, this would have been one of your biggest puzzles.

There's another side to this same problem. Scientists in the 1700s also knew that if you heated certain chemicals, such as iron powder or mercury, they would change appearance and get heavier! It seemed that new matter was being created as they heated the metals.

It took one of the world's great scientists, Antoine-Laurent Lavoisier, to figure out what was happening. And it is the Frenchman Lavoisier who is given credit for first stating the law of conservation of matter.

Before Lavoisier, scientists explained that objects lost weight when they burned because they combined with a substance in the air called phlogiston. Phlogiston was supposed to have negative weight, so a burning substance that combined with it would get lighter instead of heavier. Metals were supposed to give off phlogiston when heated, which explained why they got heavier. The trouble was, nobody had ever seen phlogiston or been able to collect it in a laboratory.

Lavoisier realized that the reason no one could find any phlogiston was because it wasn't there. He discovered that when things burn, they combine with oxygen, a gas in the air. Sometimes this burning creates other gases. The gases blow away, leaving only a little bit of ash. It might look as though matter has been destroyed, but it has actually changed form, become a gas, and entered the atmosphere. If you carefully trapped and weighed all the gases that were produced when a sheet of paper burned, you would find that all the matter from that paper still existed.

Lavoisier heated measured amounts of mercury and iron in closed containers and noted that they changed to rustlike substances. These reddish substances (oxides)

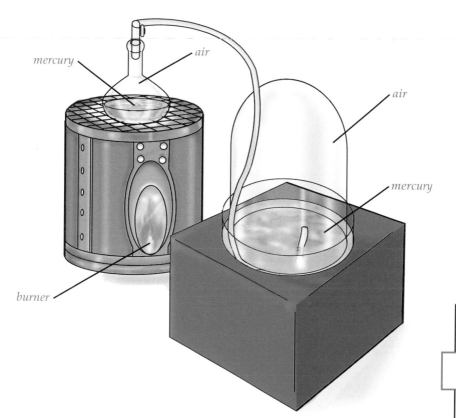

mercury

air

air

mercury

burner

Lavoisier heated mercury in a sealed container to prove that matter is neither created nor destroyed.

weighed more than the original metals. But there was also less air inside the closed containers. The amount of air that had been used up was equal to the amount of weight that the metals had gained. Lavoisier realized that no new matter had been created. Instead, the metals had combined with a portion of the air, which Lavoisier called oxygen. After many experiments, Lavoisier was sure that, while substances might change form or combine with other substances, matter could not be created or destroyed in ordinary chemical reactions.

Of course, when you mix vinegar and baking soda,

nothing is created or destroyed. The two chemicals react with each other and form other substances, including carbon dioxide gas. The same amount of material is still there, it has simply changed form.

Why was the law of conservation of matter so important? If scientists knew matter couldn't be created or destroyed, they could weigh their chemicals carefully, conduct their experiments, and figure out how elements combine to form various compounds. Only after Lavoisier and others realized that matter couldn't be created or destroyed could chemistry become an exact science. For this and other great contributions, Lavoisier is usually known as the founder of modern chemistry.

CHAPTER 2

How the Elements Combine—
The Law of Definite
Proportions and
Gay-Lussac's Law

Suppose you broke a stone into smaller and smaller pieces. How far could you go before you reached the smallest possible piece of material? And when the rock was finally broken into its smallest parts, what would be left?

Just what is matter made of? In ancient times, philosophers thought that everything on earth was compos[ ]
just four elements: earth, air, fire, and water. They believed that everything around them was made of those four substances, combined in different proportions.

In the 1700s, chemists realized that our planet was made of more than earth, air, fire, and water. But the idea of elements remained. After experimenting with many different materials, chemists found that most things they tested could be broken down into other substances. But they also found a small number of special substances that could never be broken down into anything else. These substances became known as elements. By the late 1700s, chemists had identified about twenty-five elements, including gold, silver, copper, iron, lead, sulfur, hydrogen, oxygen, and nitrogen.

Elements are the building blocks of all the other substances on earth, called compounds. For example, iron and oxygen combine to form a reddish powder called iron oxide, or rust. Hydrogen and oxygen combine to form the compound water. Calcium, carbon, and oxygen combine to form calcium carbonate, or chalk. Chemists can make iron oxide or water or calcium carbonate in their laboratories by mixing the correct elements together and then heating them or by following some other procedure.

Chemists can also reverse the process, separating compounds into their elements. For example, iron oxide can be heated in a furnace until its two elements separate. Oxygen is released as a gas, leaving pure metallic iron in the container that held the rust.

There is something special about the way the elements combine with one another to form compounds. You can't just mix elements together in any amount to form compounds. The elements combine only in regular proportions by weight.

For example, 1 gram of hydrogen gas will always combine with exactly 8 grams of oxygen gas to form 9 grams of water. Hydrogen and oxygen always combine to form water in the proportion of 1 to 8 by weight. If there is extra oxygen or extra hydrogen in the reaction, it will be left over. If you try combining 1 gram of hydrogen with 12 grams of oxygen, the result will still be 9 grams of water, with 4 grams of oxygen left over.

All other chemical reactions work the same way. Chemical elements always combine with one another in certain definite proportions. Copper and oxygen combine to form a compound called cupric oxide. Cupric oxide always has 4 grams of copper to every 1 gram of oxygen. Copper combines with carbon and oxygen to form a compound called copper carbonate. Copper carbonate always has 16 grams of copper to every 12 grams of oxygen and 3 grams of carbon.

The French chemist Joseph-Louis Proust was the first to notice that chemicals always combine in this very regular way. He experimented with many different compounds. In every reaction, the elements always combined with each other in regular amounts. If he used too much of one element, the extra would be left over. In 1797, as a result of his experiments, Proust stated his *law of definite proportions:* Elements always combine in definite proportions by weight.

Although it was Proust who first stated the law of definite proportions, it was the English chemist John Dalton who discovered what the law meant. Elements always combine in definite proportions because each element is made up of many tiny, indivisible particles, each with a definite size and weight. Dalton called these smallest particles atoms. If 4 grams of copper always combine with 1 gram of oxygen to make cupric oxide, Dalton reasoned, the smallest particles of copper must be four times heavier than the smallest particles of oxygen. If you try to use more than 1 gram of oxygen to combine with 4 grams of copper in the reaction, there won't be enough copper atoms to combine with the extra oxygen. Some oxygen will be left over.

In 1808, Dalton declared that every element is made up of atoms. Atoms are the smallest possible particles of each element. They are much too small to be seen, even with a microscope. Dalton believed that all the atoms of a certain element must be exactly alike. The reason each element is different, he said, is because its atoms are different from those of other elements. The atoms of one element all have the same weight.

And the atoms of different elements have different weights. Dalton and his fellow chemists pictured atoms as tiny balls with some sort of glue or hooks that allow them to combine with other atoms to form compounds.

Hydrogen is the lightest element. Dalton compared the weights of all the other known elements to the weight of hydrogen. He calculated an atomic weight for each known element. Dalton's calculations of atomic weights were not perfect, but they were useful in explaining why the elements always combine in definite proportions.

Dalton knew that under different conditions, some elements combine with others in more than one way. For example, carbon and oxygen can combine to form two different gases. In one gas, the proportion of carbon to oxygen is 3 to 8. In the other gas, the proportion is 3 to 4.

Copper can also combine with oxygen in two different ways. When these two elements combine in the proportion 4 to 1, the result is one compound. When they combine in the proportion of 8 to 1, a very different chemical compound is formed. How can that be?

Dalton realized that when elements combine with each other in several different ways, the law of definite proportions still holds true. Elements still combine in certain proportions. It is just that several different proportions are sometimes possible. Dalton called this the *law of multiple proportions.*

Dalton showed that his idea of atoms explained the law of multiple proportions very well. If one atom of carbon combines with one atom of oxygen, the proportion of their weights will be 3 to 4. The gas produced is carbon monoxide (the prefix *mono-* means "one").

If the number of atoms of oxygen is doubled, the proportion of carbon to oxygen will be 3 to 8. Then there will be two atoms of oxygen for each carbon atom. The gas produced in this reaction is carbon dioxide (the prefix *di-*

means "two"). The law of multiple proportions simply says that atoms can combine with one another in different ways, but they still always combine in definite proportions.

About the same time, the French chemist Joseph-Louis Gay-Lussac made a discovery that strongly supported Dalton's atomic ideas. Gay-Lussac was interested in the chemical reactions between different gases. For example, hydrogen gas and oxygen gas combine to form water. And water can be separated into the two gases, hydrogen and oxygen.

Water is separated by passing an electric current through it. This process is called electrolysis. Gay-Lussac measured the volume of gases produced in the electrolysis of water. (The volume of a gas is the amount of space it occupies.) He noticed that when water is separated into the two gases that compose it, the volume (not the weight) of hydrogen is exactly twice the volume of oxygen. For every liter of oxygen that is produced, there will be 2 liters of hydrogen.

The hydrogen gas from the electrolysis of water takes up exactly twice as much space as the oxygen. So Gay-Lussac reasoned that there had to be twice as many atoms of hydrogen as there were atoms of oxygen in the other container. Each water molecule was broken apart into two atoms of hydrogen and one atom of oxygen.

When you break water apart, you get twice as much hydrogen as oxygen. But there are twice as many hydrogen atoms too. So in equal volumes of the gases, there have to be equal numbers of particles. That discovery became known as *Gay-Lussac's law*. It is also known as *Avogadro's law*, after the Italian chemist Amedeo Avogadro, who also studied how gases combine to form compounds.

Gay-Lussac found that other chemical reactions between gases follow the same rule: In chemical reactions, gases always combine in simple proportions by volume.

Hydrogen and oxygen combine in the proportion 2 to 1 to form water. Ammonia is made up of one atom of nitrogen and three atoms of hydrogen. If ammonia is broken up into its component elements, there will be 3 liters of hydrogen for every 1 liter of nitrogen.

Changes in temperature or pressure change the volume of gas in a container. So temperature and pressure must remain constant for Gay-Lussac's law to be true. With that idea included, Gay-Lussac's law is stated like this: If pressure and temperature remain constant, equal volumes of gas contain equal numbers of gas particles. Knowing Gay-Lussac's law helped chemists determine the exact composition of many compounds that are made with gaseous elements like oxygen, hydrogen, or nitrogen. But more important, Gay-Lussac's law was evidence that Dalton was right when he said that all elements are composed of atoms.

You can see Gay-Lussac's law in action by doing a fairly simple experiment. In this experiment, you will use electrolysis to separate water into the two elements that it is composed of, hydrogen and oxygen. Because this experiment involves a tiny explosion, you should try it only when an adult is available to help.

You will need a lantern battery, some insulated wire, a deep baking pan, two test tubes or very small glasses (both the same size), table salt, and two small aluminum nails. You should be able to find these items at home or at a hardware store.

Fill the baking pan about two-thirds full with water. Pour one-fourth teaspoon of table salt (sodium chloride) into the water and stir until the salt dissolves. Adding salt improves the water's ability to conduct electricity. Strip the insulation off both ends of two pieces of wire. Wrap one end of each piece of wire around an aluminum nail. Place the nails in the water at opposite ends of the baking pan. These two metal pieces are called electrodes.

Put one test tube in the pan and fill it completely with water. Turn it upside down underwater so that none of the water in the tube escapes. Carefully put the glass tube over one of the electrodes. Repeat the same process with the other tube, placing it over the other electrode. Connect the other ends of the wires to the battery terminals. Soon you should start to see bubbles of gas forming on the electrodes.

The gas bubbling from the positive electrode is oxygen, and the gas on the negative electrode is hydrogen. The bubbles of gas will gradually fill up the test tubes, forcing the water out. When the tube of hydrogen is completely full, look at the tube that is collecting the oxygen. It should be exactly half full.

Remember that Gay-Lussac's law says that equal numbers of gas molecules will occupy equal volumes, if pressure and temperature remain constant. In your experiment, the pressures and temperatures of the two test tubes are equal. There is twice as much hydrogen as there is oxygen.

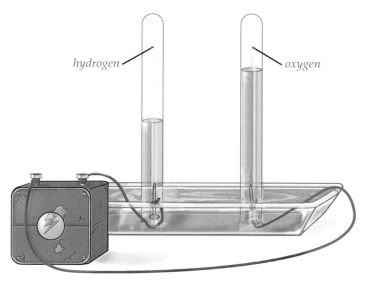

Water can be separated into hydrogen and oxygen gases using simple equipment.

hydrogen

oxygen

That tells us water is composed of two hydrogen atoms for every oxygen atom.

How can we be certain which gases we have collected? We can test them. Hydrogen and oxygen are both odorless, colorless gases. Both gases you have produced meet that test.

Oxygen sustains burning. Tightly cover or cork the mouth of the test tube over the positive electrode while it is still underwater. Take the tube out of the water. Light a toothpick with a match. When it is burning well, blow it out. Quickly uncover the tube of gas and poke the glowing toothpick in. Be careful not to get it wet as you do. If you have collected oxygen, the toothpick will glow brightly and may even burst back into flame!

Hydrogen has a different property. It burns rapidly in air. Tightly seal the other tube underwater and remove it from the pan. Light another toothpick. Hydrogen is very light, so this time hold the tube of gas upside down. That will prevent the gas from escaping when you open the tube. Uncover the tube and quickly put the burning toothpick to its mouth. You should hear a popping sound as the hydrogen you have collected explodes.

Dalton's ideas, supported by the findings of Gay-Lussac, Avogadro, and others, formed the basis of modern chemistry: Each element is made of vast numbers of tiny atoms, far too small for us to see. The atoms of each element combine with atoms of other elements to form the millions of compounds that our world is made of.

More recently, scientists studying the light from distant stars have found that the very same elements that make up the earth make up the rest of the universe as well. Throughout the universe, atoms of the different elements combine with one another in definite proportions, just as Proust, Dalton, Gay-Lussac, and others showed us almost two hundred years ago.

CHAPTER 3

Mendeleyev's Periodic Law

Elements are the building blocks of the universe. Each element is different from every other element. All the substances found on earth, and everywhere else in the universe, are composed of individual elements or combinations of elements.

Each element is made up of atoms. The atoms of each element are all alike and are different from the atoms of every other element. John Dalton showed that the atoms of each element have their own particular atomic weight. And, of course, each element has its own unique set of properties.

By 1860, chemists had identified and studied over sixty different elements. But as chemists studied the elements, they noticed each element has similarities to some of the other elements.

There are many different ways that elements can be similar. For example, some elements are gases. Others are metals. Some, like hydrogen, oxygen, sodium, and chlorine, are very reactive. They combine rapidly and easily in many chemical reactions. Some of these are so reactive that they are never found on earth in their uncombined pure form. Other elements, like gold, platinum, and nitrogen, are more inert. They don't combine so easily with other elements. Those elements are found here on earth in their elemental form, like gold nuggets or nitrogen gas.

Scientists always look for patterns in nature. As more and more elements were discovered, it began to look as if there must be some sort of pattern among the elements. But what was that pattern?

The first thing that chemists looked at was atomic weight. Dalton had shown that the atoms of different elements are different in weight. Chemists carefully calculated the atomic weight of each element. Since oxygen is a very common element that combines with most other elements, it was used as the standard measure of weight. All other elements were weighed by comparing them to the weight of oxygen.

All the known chemical elements could then be arranged in order by weight. Once that was done, chemists began examining the physical and chemical properties of the elements, looking for a pattern.

The chemical properties of the elements were most important in this search. All the elements known at that time react with other elements to form compounds. But each element combines with others only in certain ways. Chemists gave each element a particular combining number, or valence, based on the way it joins with other elements.

Here are just a few examples: One oxygen atom combines with two hydrogen atoms to form water. So each hydrogen atom is said to have a valence of 1, and the oxygen atom has a valence of 2. That is because the one oxygen

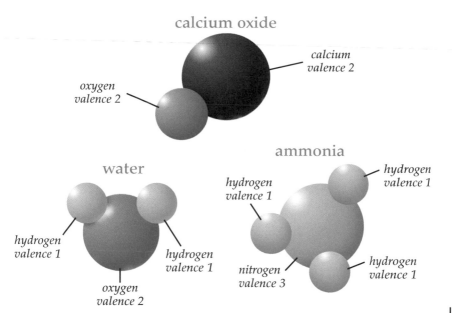

calcium oxide

calcium
valence 2

oxygen
valence 2

ammonia

water

hydrogen
valence 1

hydrogen
valence 1

hydrogen
valence 1

hydrogen
valence 1

hydrogen
valence 1

nitrogen
valence 3

oxygen
valence 2

Valence numbers are based on the proportions in which different
elements combine with one another.

atom can combine with two hydrogens. One atom of oxygen will combine with one atom of calcium to form calcium
oxide. So the calcium atom, like the oxygen, must have a
valence of 2. One nitrogen atom combines with three
hydrogen atoms to form ammonia. Since each hydrogen
atom has a combining power of 1, then nitrogen's valence
must be 3.

On the next page is a list, by weight, of the
eighteen elements known in 1860. The valence of each is
also shown.

But valence is only one of many properties each element
has. How did all those properties fit into one simple pattern?
One chemist thought that all the elements with similar properties could be placed in groups of three. Another scientist
thought every sixteenth element might be similar. Many different numerical arrangements were tried. But in every
scheme, some elements just didn't fit properly.

Element	Valence
Hydrogen	1
Lithium	1
Beryllium	2
Boron	3
Carbon	4
Nitrogen	3
Oxygen	2
Fluorine	1
Sodium	1
Magnesium	2
Aluminum	3
Silicon	4
Phosphorus	3
Sulfur	2
Chlorine	1
Potassium	1
Calcium	2
Titanium	3

In 1866, John Newlands suggested the elements followed a pattern like a musical scale. The combining numbers, or valences, seemed to repeat themselves in groups of seven. Newlands published a chart of elements arranged in this pattern. The chart worked beautifully for the lighter elements listed above. But the pattern fell apart with the heavier elements. Newlands was on the right track, but he had not solved the puzzle.

In 1869, Dmitri Mendeleyev, a Russian chemist, finally won the honor of discovering the pattern of the elements.

Mendeleyev realized the valences of the elements are their most important chemical property. They show exactly how each element reacts with all other elements. Mendeleyev arranged the elements according to their atomic weight. He then grouped them according to their valences. When he arranged the elements in this way, he discovered that their chemical and physical properties showed a periodic, or repeating, pattern.

Newlands and the other chemists had tried to find a "magic number" of elements that repeated again and again through the list of known elements. But Mendeleyev didn't try to force the elements into a regular numerical pattern.

When Mendeleyev got to the fourth repetition of the periodic cycle, he found a large number of elements in the list that had a valence of 3. Mendeleyev simply made the period longer. Those "extra" elements all had to be included before the cycle continued. The same thing was true for the fifth period and the sixth period. Because he grouped the elements by their properties, rather than any particular number, Mendeleyev simply widened his chart to make room for the additional elements that belonged in those groups.

Mendeleyev's discovery can be stated as a law: When arranged in order of atomic weight, the elements periodically repeat similar physical and chemical properties. This is known as the *periodic law.* Mendeleyev's chart of the elements, which shows this repetition of properties, is known as the periodic table. The chart itself is actually the most complete statement of Mendeleyev's law. Mendeleyev's original table, which included all the elements known to chemists of his time, is shown on the next two pages.

Moving from left to right and down the page, the elements in Mendeleyev's chart are in order by atomic weight. Each row across the page is called a period. Each period represents one complete repetition of similar chemical and physical properties.

Each column of elements in the periodic table is a group of elements with similar properties. These groups of elements are sometimes called families of elements.

For example, the elements in the leftmost column are known as the alkali metals family. This family includes hydrogen, lithium, sodium, potassium, rubidium, and

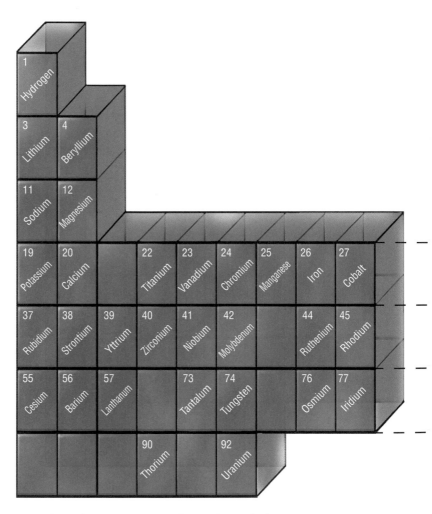

Mendeleyev arranged all the elements known in his time into a chart called the periodic table.

cesium. These elements are all metallic; even hydrogen acts like a metal at very low temperatures. They all have a valence of 1. These elements are all so chemically active that, except for hydrogen gas, they are never found on earth in their pure form. They are always combined with other elements in compounds.

The second column is another group of metals, known as the alkaline earth metals. They have a valence of 2. They are also very reactive, although not quite as reactive as the elements in the first column.

In the last column of the chart is a family of elements known as the halogens. The halogens are nonmetals that are also very chemically active. In fact, fluorine is the most reactive element of all. It is so reactive that it is almost impossible to produce and keep fluorine in its elemental form. It will even react with glass! The halogens also include the elements chlorine, bromine, and iodine. They all have a valence of 1 and react strongly with metals. They have strong, unpleasant odors and can be quite poisonous.

As Mendeleyev arranged the elements by their properties, he found several places where an element seemed to be missing. Mendeleyev was so convinced his periodic law was correct that he left empty spaces in his chart for undiscovered elements that he thought should be there.

Mendeleyev was familiar with the properties of the other elements in the family where he thought the missing elements belonged. He knew that the missing elements would have similar properties. So Mendeleyev made a prediction. He predicted that four new elements would be found. He predicted what the properties of those elements would be. If those elements were found, they would prove that Mendeleyev's periodic law was correct. If they were not, then Mendeleyev was wrong, and some other arrangement was needed to describe the properties of the elements.

In 1874, five years after Mendeleyev first published his periodic table, the first discovery was made. A French chemist found one of the missing elements. It was named gallium. Its atomic weight and physical and chemical properties matched Mendeleyev's predictions almost exactly!

In 1878, the element scandium was discovered. It matched another of the blank spots that Mendeleyev had left in his periodic table. And in 1886, the third element that Mendeleyev had predicted was found. It was named germanium. These discoveries clearly proved that Mendeleyev's periodic law was correct.

The fourth element that Mendeleyev had predicted wasn't found until 1937. It was named technetium, because it was produced in a laboratory. Technetium is radioactive and quickly decays into other elements. It has such a short lifetime that it no longer exists naturally on the earth. But it does exist. Mendeleyev's predictions had all proved true!

The reason the elements follow this periodic pattern was not found until fifty years after Mendeleyev's discovery. The laws that describe the structure of atoms, known as the principles of quantum mechanics, explain why the elements form groups with similar properties.

Since Mendeleyev's time, a number of additional elements have been added to the periodic chart. One whole family of elements known as the inert gases was discovered in the late 1800s. These gases were difficult to find because they don't react at all with other elements. Helium, argon, neon, krypton, xenon, and radon are all members of this family of elements.

Two other large groups of elements were also discovered. One group is known as the lanthanides, or rare earth elements. They are found in the earth's crust only in tiny quantities. The other group is made up of radioactive elements. They are known as actinides.

Although all these elements were found after the periodic law was discovered, they fit nicely into the pattern that Mendeleyev found. The current periodic table is shown on the next two pages. It includes 115 elements. They all follow Mendeleyev's periodic law.

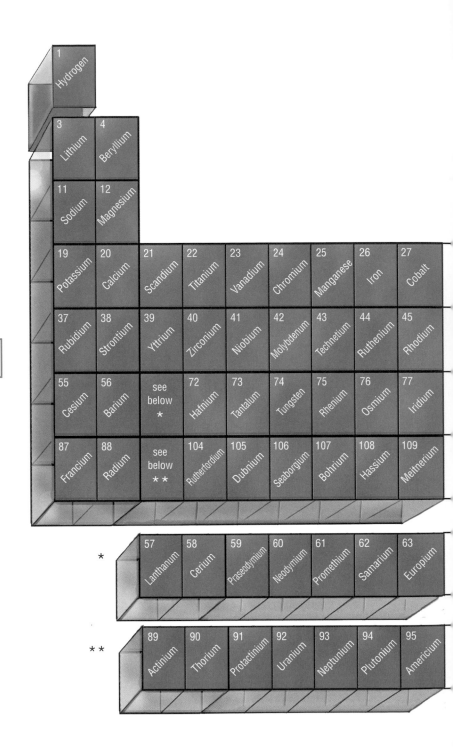

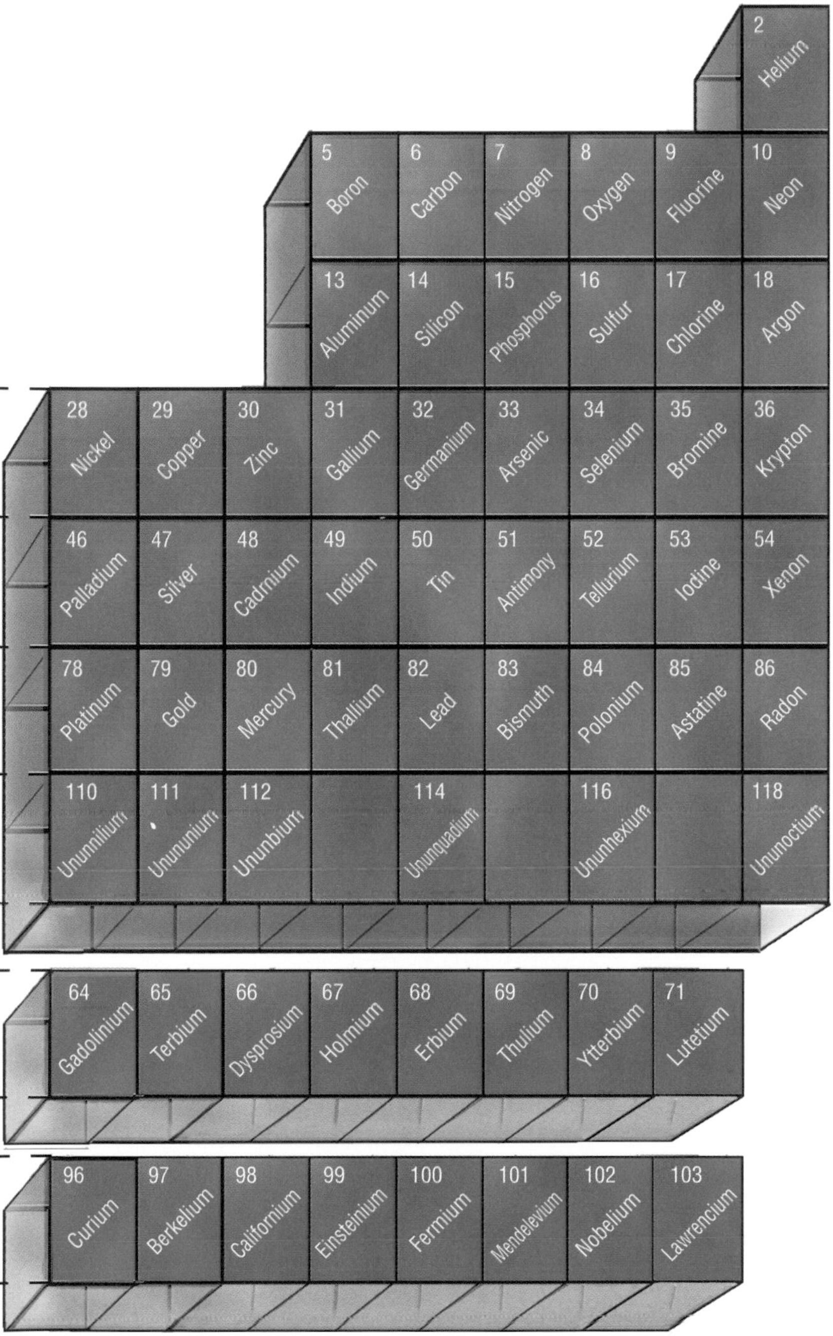

2 Helium
5 Boron
6 Carbon
7 Nitrogen
8 Oxygen
9 Fluorine
10 Neon
13 Aluminum
14 Silicon
15 Phosphorus
16 Sulfur
17 Chlorine
18 Argon
28 Nickel
29 Copper
30 Zinc
31 Gallium
32 Germanium
33 Arsenic
34 Selenium
35 Bromine
36 Krypton
46 Palladium
47 Silver
48 Cadmium
49 Indium
50 Tin
51 Antimony
52 Tellurium
53 Iodine
54 Xenon
78 Platinum
79 Gold
80 Mercury
81 Thallium
82 Lead
83 Bismuth
84 Polonium
85 Astatine
86 Radon
110 Ununnilium
111 Unununium
112 Ununbium
114 Ununquadium
116 Ununhexium
118 Ununoctium
64 Gadolinium
65 Terbium
66 Dysprosium
67 Holmium
68 Erbium
69 Thulium
70 Ytterbium
71 Lutetium
96 Curium
97 Berkelium
98 Californium
99 Einsteinium
100 Fermium
101 Mendelevium
102 Nobelium
103 Lawrencium

CHAPTER

Every time we lift an object, move it, push it, or carry it, we are doing work. And each time we do work, we use energy, or force. If we use our muscles, that energy comes from the food we eat. If we use a machine, the energy comes from oil, gasoline, coal, electricity, or some other energy source. Even a tree needs energy to lift its water and minerals high above the ground. The energy for that work comes from the sun.

Without energy no work can be done. In fact, scientists define energy as the ability to do work. But what happens to energy after its work is completed? Is it "used up"? Does it disappear or just return to where it came from? Does it become a part of the object it was used on, or does it change into something else?

Scientists have discovered that energy is conserved.

Energy may change forms, but it is neither created nor destroyed. That rule is known as the *law of conservation of energy*.

Discovering this law wasn't the work of a single researcher. Many famous scientists contributed to the understanding of heat and the other forms of energy. Several different scientists have been given credit for first discovering the law itself. One of the two most often named is the English scientist James Prescott Joule. His experiments about energy transformations were published in 1843. The second scientist most often named is the German scientist Hermann von Helmholtz who, is credited with writing the law in its final form in 1847.

The story of the law of conservation of energy begins in the late 1600s with a Dutch scientist named Christiaan Huygens. Huygens wondered what happened to the energy of moving objects when they collided. He imagined what would happen if perfectly hard billiard balls bumped into one another. He realized that the force of one ball would be transferred to the other balls as it hit them.

In the game of pool, a player is allowed to hit only the white cue ball. The cue ball then hits other balls, transferring its energy to them. The motion of the cue ball is transferred to the ball it hits. If the player has aimed correctly, the transferred energy will send the other ball exactly where the player wants it to go.

The energy of motion is called kinetic energy. Huygens concluded that kinetic energy could be transferred completely from one ball to another if the two balls were perfectly hard. The total amount of energy would be conserved—no energy would be lost in the transfer.

Of course, there is no such thing as a perfectly hard ball. When real balls collide, kinetic energy is not completely transferred from one ball to the other. Some energy is lost to friction. Some is absorbed by the balls themselves as they

The First Law of Thermodynamics

are temporarily dented when they collide. Some straight-line motion may be converted into spinning motion.

It wasn't until the middle of the 1800s that scientists were finally sure that the total amount of energy in any action stays the same. None of the energy is really "lost." It just changes forms. It may be changed from the energy of motion to heat or from heat to light or from electricity to motion. But no new energy is created, and none is lost. That is what the law of conservation of energy says: Energy may change forms, but it can neither be created nor destroyed.

Energy comes in several different forms. It can take the form of heat, light, electricity, kinetic energy (movement), chemical energy (like the energy in coal, gasoline, or food), or nuclear energy. The law of conservation of energy tells us

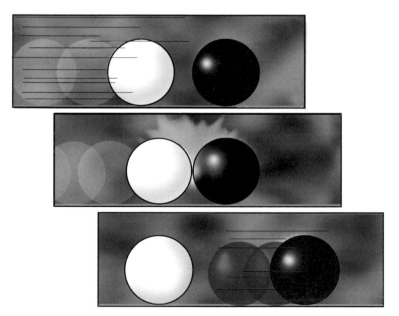

A moving cue ball transfers its kinetic energy to a second ball as it strikes it.

that energy can be converted from any of these forms to any other form. It is still energy, and none of it disappears when it is converted.

In the 1700s, scientists were not sure that heat was a kind of energy. Most thought that heat was a weightless, invisible fluid, which they called caloric. However, in 1798 Benjamin Thompson, known as Count Rumford, proved that caloric doesn't exist and heat is just another form of energy.

Rumford studied the heat produced when cannon barrels were drilled out. The more the metal was drilled, the more heat was produced. The metal never seemed to run out of heat as it was drilled. Rumford measured the heat and proved that it couldn't all have come from the caloric in the little pile of metal shavings that the drilling produced. Instead, it had to be produced by the friction created as the drill spun around in the cannon. Rumford's experiment proved that heat is not a substance after all. It is a form of energy.

In the early 1800s, James Prescott Joule began studying how the energy of motion changes into heat. Joule and his fellow scientists lived at a time when steam engines were being used in many industries. Wherever he looked, Joule could see examples of energy being converted from one form to another. Steam engines got their energy by burning coal, a source of chemical energy. The engines turned the chemical energy into the motion of pistons, wheels, and pulleys. That energy was then used to do work of many different kinds. Steam engines could even generate electrical energy. Joule realized that any form of energy can be transformed into any other form.

You can easily transform chemical energy to mechanical energy to heat energy using nothing but your own two hands. Put the palms of your hands together and rub them vigorously for thirty seconds. You will feel quite a bit of heat. Your muscles transform the chemical energy of the

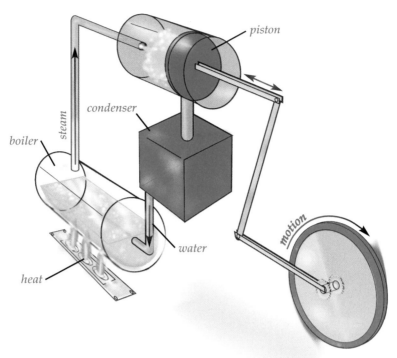

labels: piston, condenser, boiler, steam, water, heat, motion

A steam engine changes the heat energy of boiling water into mechanical energy, which is then used to do work.

food you eat into motion. The friction between your two hands transforms their kinetic energy into heat.

A similar thing happens when you hammer a nail. Try hammering a large nail most of the way into a block of wood. Then feel the head of the nail. It will be warm. Some of the energy of your hammering has pushed the nail into the wood, and some of it has turned into heat energy, warming the nail, the wood, and even the air around you.

One way to start a fire is to focus the sun's rays on a pile of dry tinder with a magnifying glass. In this case, light energy is converted into enough heat energy to start a fire.

Joule designed a series of clever experiments to show that when energy changes form, none of it disappears. In his most famous experiment, he attached a weight on a cable to a paddle wheel. Joule knew exactly how much energy the weight used as it fell. As the paddle wheel turned, its motion heated the water. Joule carefully measured the change in water temperature. The amount of extra heat in the water exactly equaled the energy of the falling weight. The form of the energy was changed from motion to heat, but no energy was lost.

Because Joule and his fellow researchers concentrated on studying the movement of heat energy, the branch of physics they studied is called thermodynamics. The prefix *thermo-* means "heat," and *dynamics* is the study of motion.

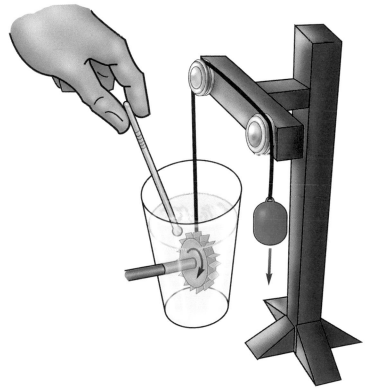

As the weight falls, the paddle wheel turns and the temperature of the water rises.

The law of conservation of energy is also known as the *first law of thermodynamics.* Because of James Prescott Joule's contributions to the study of energy, the metric unit used to measure work is named the joule in his honor.

Machines do work by converting one form of energy to another. For example, a car converts the chemical energy in gasoline to kinetic energy (motion). The law of conservation of energy tells us a machine must have a source of energy. It cannot create its own. And a machine cannot supply more power than it gets from its energy source. When the energy runs out, the machine stops.

The same rule is true for living things. Plants get the power they need to live and grow from the sun's energy. Without that energy supply, plants will die. They cannot produce their own energy. Animals must eat food to supply themselves with energy for life. They too will die if their energy supply runs out.

Energy can neither be created nor destroyed. So the energy of any system, machine, or creature must balance out in the end. No energy can be lost or gained. That means it is possible to trace the energy "budget" of any object to see where the energy comes from and where it goes.

When a person goes on a diet, he uses the law of conservation of energy to change his personal energy budget. When a person eats, he takes in chemical energy in the form of food. The amount of energy he takes in is measured in calories. Those calories are then converted to energy for walking, running, talking, thinking, and so on. They are also converted to heat as the body does its work. The more food a person takes in, the more energy he must convert to keep his energy budget balanced. If a person takes in more energy than he can use, the extra gets stored as fat.

A dieter eats less, and so he takes in less food energy. If he keeps up a normal level of activity, he will get the remaining energy he needs by burning the fat stored in his body. As the fat is converted to energy, the dieter loses weight.

Even the earth as a whole has its own energy budget. The earth receives almost all of its energy from the sun in the form of light. Some of that energy reflects back into space. Some turns into heat, which warms the earth. The earth later radiates that heat back into space. Some solar energy is captured by plants and is turned into chemical energy by their leaves. Some sunlight provides energy to evaporate water, form clouds, and produce rain. But the totals all balance out. The law of conservation of energy tells us that no matter what we do, we cannot end up with more energy than we started with—or less.

The same law holds true for the whole universe. The universe has a certain total amount of energy. The total energy of the universe is enormous, of course. There are billions of stars burning with vast storehouses of energy. But the energy in the universe is not limitless. No new energy is being created anywhere in the universe, and none is being lost. It is just endlessly changing its forms.

CHAPTER 5

The Second Law of Thermodynamics— Entropy

Thermodynamics is the science of energy transformations. The first law of thermodynamics tells us that energy cannot be created or destroyed, but it can be transformed. The *second law of thermodynamics* tells us what happens in those transformations.

Here's an experiment to try: Fill a coffee cup with hot water. Measure its temperature. Then place it on a table and leave it there for two hours. When you return, check the temperature again. It will be much cooler, of course. We know the heat energy in that hot water couldn't just disappear. The first law of thermodynamics tells us that. So where did that energy go?

It is in the air of the room. The heat of the water was gradually transferred to the molecules in the surrounding air. If you had a very sensitive thermometer, you could even measure the slight rise in air temperature that resulted from the heat transfer. The energy of that hot water still exists, but it has spread out into the room.

Try to put that energy back into the cup of water. Collect the spread-out heat energy from the air and bring the water in the cup back to its original temperature.

It can't be done! The energy still exists, but to collect it and put it back in a concentrated form is impossible. At least it is impossible without using lots more energy to collect it.

That impossible experiment is an example of the second law of thermodynamics. The scientists who first stated the second law of thermodynamics were Rudolf Clausius of Germany and William Thomson, Lord Kelvin, of England. However, many others also contributed to the under-standing of this law, which was first published in 1850.

There are several different ways of stating the second law of thermodynamics. One way of saying it is this: In any energy transformation, heat always flows from areas of higher concentration to areas of lower concentration. That means that heat always moves from hotter areas to cooler ones. The heat energy in any system has a tendency to "spread out" until finally everything is the same temperature.

To see this law in action, you will need a glass and a small pitcher, hot and cold water, some red food coloring, and a large spoon. Fill the glass half full of cold water. Pour a few ounces of very hot water into the pitcher, and then color it with six to eight drops of the red dye. The red dye will show where the heat is concentrated in the water. The clear water represents the area of less heat.

Place the spoon just at the surface of the cold water in the glass. Gently pour the hot water onto the spoon. If you pour slowly and carefully, the hot water will form a separate layer on top of the cold water.

As time passes, the hot water gradually mixes with the

Pouring hot water gently over the cold water creates two temperature layers.

cold water. After a while, the dye will be completely mixed into pale pink water. Along with the dye, the heat in the water will be spread evenly throughout the glass.

Another way of stating the second law of thermodynamics is: In any energy transformation some useful energy will be lost and turned into unrecoverable heat.

Heat is the least useful form energy can take. The second law of thermodynamics tells us that whenever energy is put to use, some of it will be turned into waste heat. Waste heat is energy that can no longer do useful work. The word for this loss of useful, organized energy is entropy. The second law of thermodynamics is also known as the *law of entropy.*

The law of entropy means energy transformations are

not reversible. You can't reassemble a piece of firewood after it has been burned. The laws of conservation of matter and energy tell us that all the energy and material still exist. But they have spread out. You can't collect all that matter and energy and put the log back together again. It's like trying to unscramble an egg and put it back in the shell. It can't be done.

Consider what happens when you run a lawn mower. The lawn mower gets its power from the chemical energy in gasoline. As the gasoline burns in the engine, it is converted to mechanical energy. The blades and wheels of the mower turn, doing useful work. But not all of the energy from the gasoline is turned into useful work. Much of it is turned into heat. Heat escapes into the air with the hot exhaust gases. More heat radiates into the air from the hot engine. All that heat is "wasted" energy. It does no useful work. It just spreads out into the air, making the air slightly warmer. It still exists, but nothing more can be done with it.

The same thing always happens when machines use energy. No machine can be perfectly efficient. That means no machine can use 100 percent of its energy to do work. Some energy always leaks away as heat.

This fact was first discovered by the French engineer Sadi Carnot. He was trying to calculate just how efficient the perfect steam engine could be. Steam engines produce power when hot steam pushes against pistons. To keep the power coming, this motion must be repeated over and over again. But that means the same steam can't remain in the piston's cylinder. The "used" steam must be removed, to allow the engine to recycle for another burst of power. The exhaust steam must then be cooled back into water and returned to the boiler to produce more steam.

Carnot realized that in order to work, the steam engine must lose some heat as the steam cools. It also loses energy

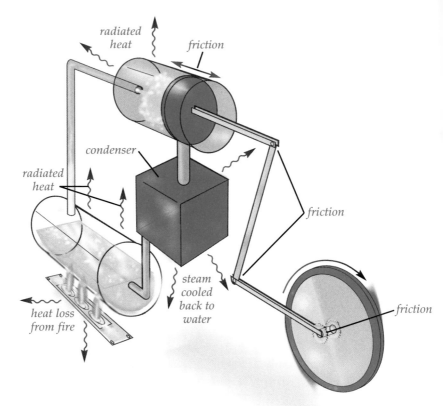

Most of the heat energy in a steam engine is wasted. Only a small fraction of it is converted to useful work.

as heat "leaks" from the hotter portions of the machinery to the cooler ones. It loses more heat as smoke from the burning coal escapes up the chimney. It loses still more heat as the parts of the machinery rub against each other, producing friction. Even under perfect conditions, much of the energy of the burning coal is lost as waste heat.

We can see examples of entropy, or the loss of useful energy, wherever energy is used. For example, a lamp wastes part of its electrical energy by producing heat as well as light. If you put your hand near a lightbulb, you can feel it. Household appliances like blenders, vacuum cleaners, washing machines, and refrigerators also produce heat as they work. Automobiles produce useless heat in their exhaust and in the friction of their moving parts. Even a baseball thrown in the air loses some of its energy to the heat of friction as it rubs against the molecules of the air.

Living creatures are also subject to the law of entropy. Muscles produce heat as they work. Anyone who has ever run a race knows that. After you run, you're hot. As you cool off, the heat gradually spreads out into the air around you.

The laws of thermodynamics prove that a "perpetual motion" machine can never be built. For hundreds of years, people have tried to design a machine that could run forever under its own power. Unfortunately, it is completely hopeless. There is no way that any machine can produce the energy to keep itself running, much less create additional energy to do useful work. The first law of thermodynamics tells us energy cannot be created. And the second law of thermodynamics tells us every machine must lose energy as it works. You simply can't win when you turn energy into work. So a machine that would provide its own power to keep running forever is impossible.

The law of entropy has another interesting and even scary result. It tells us that the universe is slowly running down! Every time there is a transformation of energy, energy spreads out and becomes less concentrated. This happens in the collisions of planets, nuclear reactions in the stars, chemical reactions between atoms, the friction of two gears rubbing together, and all the other events happening throughout the universe.

The law of entropy tells us all energy in the universe will eventually level out. Everything in the universe will be at the same temperature. No more energy transformations will be possible, and all activity in the universe will come to a stop. This final state is sometimes called the heat death of the universe.

That idea does sound frightening. However, we don't really need to worry about it. The universe is still full of usable energy, so the end won't come for billions of years. In fact, scientists still don't know whether this heat death will happen at all. It depends on how much matter there is in the entire universe.

Scientists believe that our universe was first created billions of years ago in a huge explosion they call the big bang. The universe is still expanding. But if there is enough matter in the universe, gravitational force will eventually take over. The expansion of the universe will slow, stop, and then reverse. After billions of years, gravity will pull all the mass of the universe back together again to one tiny point. Then there will be another big bang, and the universe will start all over again. If that is true, then the universe expands and contracts over and over again. That would mean that the energy of the universe would recharge itself, and the heat death predicted by the law of entropy would never happen.

But perhaps there is not enough mass in the universe to stop its expansion with gravitational force. If that is the case, then the creation of the universe is a one-time event. The universe will continue expanding and cooling and the law of entropy will continue in effect. The energy level of the universe will continue to run down until, in billions of years, the universe will be evenly cold and lifeless everywhere.

Evidence seems to support the second possibility. But it's still a mystery! No one knows yet which possibility is correct. Scientists do not yet know how much matter there is in the universe. Perhaps scientists will discover another possible fate for our universe. Meanwhile, the law of entropy is in effect. Little by little, every event turns some of the universe's useful energy into useless heat.

We don't know all there is to know about the universe.

Scientists still have much to learn about the stars and planets, the atom, and the miracles of life. There are still more laws to discover and more mysteries to solve. Perhaps you may one day add your name to that list of distinguished scientists who have helped discover the secrets of the universe.

1678	**Christiaan Huygens proposes his wave theory of light**
1687	**Isaac Newton publishes his *Principia Mathematica***
1692	Witchcraft trials take place in Salem, Massachusetts
1714	**Daniel Gabriel Fahrenheit invents the mercury thermometer**
1732	Benjamin Franklin begins publishing *Poor Richard's Almanack*
1742	**Anders Celsius introduces the centigrade temperature scale**
1752	Benjamin Franklin discovers the electrical nature of lightning through his kite-flying experiment
1772	**Daniel Rutherford discovers nitrogen**
1773	Boston Tea Party
1774	**Joseph Priestley discovers oxygen**
1775-1783	American War of Independence
1776	American Declaration of Independence is written
1787	U.S. Constitution is signed
1789	George Washington becomes the first president of the United States
1790	**Antoine-Laurent Lavoisier publishes a list of 31 chemical elements**
1794	Eli Whitney patents his cotton gin

1797	Joseph-Louis Proust states the law of definite proportions
1798	Count Rumford proves that heat is a form of energy and that "caloric" doesn't exist
1799	The Rosetta Stone is discovered in Egypt
1808	John Dalton proposes that every element is made up of atoms
1811	Amedeo Avogadro proposes his gas law
1823	Charles Macintosh develops waterproof fabric in Scotland
1828	Noah Webster's *American Dictionary of the English Language* is published
1829	Louis Braille's system of writing for the blind is first published (revised in 1837)
1843	James Prescott Joule's experiments on energy transformation are published
1847	Hermann von Helmholtz writes the law of conservation of energy in its final form (first law of thermodynamics)
1848	Second law of thermodynamics is published by Rudolf Clausius
1851	Isaac Merrit Singer patents his sewing machine
1859	Charles Darwin publishes *The Origin of Species by Natural Selection*
1861-1865	American Civil War
1865	President Abraham Lincoln is assassinated
1866	John Newlands suggests that elements follow a pattern similar to a musical scale
1869	Dmitri Mendeleyev proposes his periodic law

Timeline

Amedeo Avogadro (1776–1856) was born in Turin, Italy, with the full name of Lorenzo Romano Amedeo Carlo Avogadro. He came from a well-respected family of lawyers and began his own career in the legal field at age sixteen. His deeper interest in the sciences, however, led him to begin studying math and physics in 1800. He eventually became a professor of physics. In 1811, he proposed that equal volumes of all gases, under identical conditions of temperature and pressure, contain the same number of molecules. Although this theory successfully resolved an apparent contradiction between John Dalton's and Joseph Gay-Lussac's work, it was not accepted until after Avogadro's death.

Sadi Carnot (1796–1832) came from a very politically minded French family. Carnot served his country as a military engineer, but he preferred conducting his own research as a civilian. Especially interested in steam engines, Carnot's studies of their efficiency proved that, even under ideal conditions, all machines must lose some energy in the form of heat. Carnot was not widely recognized during his lifetime. But his observations would be used to develop the second law of thermodynamics, also known as the law of entropy. He is considered one of the founders of thermodynamics.

Rudolf Clausius (1822–1888) was born in Germany to a pastor and his wife. He went to the University of Berlin planning to study history but soon switched to science. He went on to become a professor of physics. Building on the work of Sadi Carnot, Clausius played a large role in formulating the second law of thermodynamics. He was also instrumental in defining the concept of entropy. This concept unsettled many of his contemporaries because it predicted the fearsome "heat death" of the universe. In addition to his well-known work in thermodynamics, Clausius studied electrolysis and gases. He was wounded in 1870, during the Franco-Prussian War, when he and his students operated an ambulance service.

John Dalton (1766–1844) was a British scientist who began teaching when he was just twelve years old. His interests were broad, ranging from meteorology to color blindness. Color blind himself, Dalton even requested that his eyes be donated to scientific research after his death. In the area of meteorology, he was particularly interested in rainfall and atmospheric humidity. Beginning in 1787 and continuing until his death, Dalton kept a daily journal of weather observations. He recorded a total of about two hundred thousand entries. Dalton also studied gases, contributing to the theory that was eventually formulated in Charles's law. But his most famous work was his atomic theory, stated in 1808.

Joseph-Louis Gay-Lussac (1778–1850) was a French physicist and chemist who grew up during the French Revolution. Both the political turmoil in his homeland and his adventurous approach to science kept his life interesting. Gay-Lussac had a great interest in hot-air ballooning. In 1804, he reached an altitude of over four miles during one of his flights. He used these balloon excursions to observe magnetism and air composition at varying altitudes. Much of Gay-Lussac's most prominent work was done in the study of gases. Gay-Lussac also studied chemical elements and compounds quite extensively, including a few that have explosive properties.

Hermann von Helmholtz (1821–1894) was a German scientist who was most famous for being one of the primary contributors to the law of conservation of energy. He began his career as an army surgeon and physiologist, extensively studying vision, hearing, and nerve impulses. Helmholtz was especially interested in how the human senses perceive and interpret creative aspects of the outside world, such as color and music. He was an excellent pianist himself, and he used his knowledge of music to investigate the science behind harmony and hearing. Eventually Helmholtz turned more completely to the study of physics, focusing primarily on electricity and magnetism.

Christiaan Huygens (1629–1695) was born to a wealthy Dutch family in The Hague. Educated in science and mathematics, he was one of many physicists to be puzzled and intrigued by the nature of light. In 1678, Huygens proposed his wave theory of light, which was contrary to the particle theory supported by Newton. Not until well after both their deaths would the dual nature of light be discovered. Another of Huygens's great contributions to physics was his study of the pendulum and its applications to timekeeping. Huygens was interested in astronomy. His homemade telescope was a considerable improvement over those used by earlier scientists. With it, he discovered Saturn's largest moon and more clearly distinguished the shape of Saturn's rings, which were first observed by the scientist Galileo.

James Prescott Joule (1818–1889) was a British physicist. The son of a successful brewer in Manchester, England, Joule was shy and rather sickly as a child. Fortunately, his family's wealth allowed him to be educated at home by private tutors. His science and math teacher was John Dalton. Joule enjoyed physics and was particularly fascinated by heat and its relationship to energy. He even took time on his honeymoon to measure the temperature difference of water at the top and bottom of a waterfall. He extended his study of heat to include electricity, and he conducted many imaginative and careful experiments in these areas. His work led to the formulation of Joule's law on electric current and resistance. He was also a contributor to the law of conservation of energy.

Antoine-Laurent Lavoisier (1743-1794) was a French chemist who led a very full life. He first studied law, but he loved science and displayed great talent and energy for research. Recognized as one of the major founders of modern chemistry, Lavoisier was also a dedicated social reformer. As a scientist, he developed a theory of combustion, established a system for naming chemical compounds, and contributed to the law of conservation of matter. As a social activist, he studied ways to improve French agriculture, water quality, public education, and welfare. Sadly, Lavoisier's fruitful career was cut short. During the French Revolution's Reign of Terror, he was guillotined for his connection to a tax-collecting agency.

Dmitri Mendeleyev (1834-1907) was born in Siberia, Russia. His early years were rather rocky. When his father went blind, Mendeleyev's mother ran a glass factory to support their large family. A few years later, his father died and the factory burned down. Despite these troubles, Mendeleyev was an excellent student and went to Saint Petersburg to study chemistry. Later, as a university professor, he was dissatisfied with available chemistry textbooks. He decided to write his own, which became a classic. Mendeleyev's greatest achievement came about almost by chance. He had created a deck of flash cards, each card showing an atomic element and its properties. He was playing a type of solitaire with the deck when he noticed something interesting. If the cards were laid out in a particular way, elements with similar properties were grouped together. This casual observation led to the creation of Mendeleyev's periodic table.

John Newlands (1837–1898) was a British chemist who specialized in industrial chemistry. His career was slightly delayed in 1860, when he fought in Italy for that country's unification. Later in his life, he worked as chief chemist in a sugar refinery. Newlands was personally interested in the arrangement of the elements according to their properties, a great puzzle to chemists of the time. He developed a theory called the law of octaves, which stated that, when arranged by atomic weight, every eighth element in the chart tended to show similar characteristics. Newlands's idea was a step toward the puzzle's solution. It was harshly criticized at the time, however, and the periodic table later developed by Mendeleyev proved to be more accurate and complete.

Joseph-Louis Proust (1754–1826) was a French analytical chemist. He began his career as an apothecary (pharmacist) in Paris. He later moved to Spain to teach and to work in the Royal Laboratory of King Charles IV. He conducted important and productive work there. Proust returned to France during the Napoleonic Wars after his lab in Madrid was heavily damaged by Napoleon's troops. Proust extensively studied the makeup of various chemical compounds. He discovered through this analysis that the different elements in any pure substance always combine in the same proportions. This discovery became the law of definite proportions, Proust's primary contribution to science.

Benjamin Thompson was born in Woburn, Massa-
(Count Rumford) chusetts. He is important as a
(1753–1814) physicist for discovering that heat
is not a physical substance, as was
thought at the time, but actually a form of energy. In addition to this scientific achievement, Rumford had an interesting personal life. During the American War of
Independence, Rumford sided with the British, possibly
working as a spy. He left the colonies for England in 1776.
He later emigrated to Bavaria (modern-day Germany),
where among other things he worked in welfare and social
reform, invented a double boiler and a drip coffeepot, and
created a large public park in Munich. From Bavaria he
returned to England to found the Royal Institution in
London with Sir Joseph Banks. Finally he moved to France,
where he continued his scientific pursuits.

William Thomson was a British physicist with a wide
(Lord Kelvin) range of interests and talents. As the
(1824–1907) son of a mathematics professor,
Thomson was encouraged to pursue
science and began studying it at the age of ten. He eventually became a professor of physics at the University of
Glasgow, and held the post for fifty-three years. Though
Thomson studied subjects from magnetism to the tides, one
of his primary interests was heat. His work formed a great
part of the second law of thermodynamics. He was also
lucky enough to make his fortune in science, through his
work on the first operational transatlantic telegraph cable.
The success of this project brought him both the title of
baron and great wealth. In his personal life, Thomson especially loved sailing. He invented several navigational tools,
including a compass that was adopted by the British navy.

Asimov, Isaac. *Asimov's Chronology of Science and Discovery.* New York: HarperCollins, 1994.

Brown, G. I. *Scientist, Soldier, Statesman, Spy: Count Rumford: The Extraordinary Life of a Scientific Genius.* Stroud, Gloucestershire: Sutton, 1999.

Cooper, Christopher. *Matter.* New York: Dorling Kindersley, 1992.

Friedhoffer, Robert. *Physics Lab in the Home.* New York: Franklin Watts, 1997.

Henderson, Harry, and Lisa Yount. *The Scientific Revolution.* San Diego: Lucent Books, 1996.

Meadows, Jack. *The Great Scientists.* New York: Oxford University Press, 1997.

Spangenburg, Ray. *The History of Science from the Ancient Greeks to the Scientific Revolution.* New York: Facts on File, 1993.

Wilkinson, Philip, and Michael Pollard. *Scientists Who Changed the World.* New York: Chelsea House Publishers, 1994.

Wood, Robert W. *Who?: Famous Experiments for the Young Scientist.* Philadelphia: Chelsea House Publishers, 1999.

Yount, Lisa. *Antoine Lavoisier: Founder of Modern Chemistry.* Springfield, NJ: Enslow Publishers, 1997.

Websites

Center for History of Physics, sponsored by the American
    Institute of Physics
<http://www.aip.org/history/index.html>

Cool Science, sponsored by the U.S. Department of Energy
<http://www.fetc.doe.gov/coolscience/index.html>

The Franklin Institute Science Museum online
<http://www.fi.edu/tfi/welcome.html>

Kid's Castle, sponsored by the Smithsonian Institution
    Includes a science site.
<http://www.kidscastle.si.edu/>

NPR's *Sounds Like Science* site
<http://www.npr.org/programs/science/>

PBS's *A Science Odyssey* site
<http://www.pbs.org/wgbh/aso/>

Science Learning Network
<http://www.sln.org/>

Science Museum of Minnesota
<http://www.smm.org/>

For Further Reading

Adler, Irving. *The Wonders of Physics: An Introduction to the Physical World.* New York: Golden Press, 1966.

Asimov, Isaac. *Asimov's New Guide to Science.* New York: Basic Books, 1984.

_____. *The History of Physics.* New York: Walker and Co., 1966.

_____. *The Search for the Elements.* New York: Basic Books, 1962.

Chisholm, Jane, and Mary Johnson. *Usborne Introduction to Chemistry.* Tulsa, OK: Usborne, 1983.

Gamow, George. *Biography of Physics.* New York: Harper & Row, 1961.

Goldstein-Jackson, Kevin. *Experiments with Everyday Objects: Science Activities for Children, Parents and Teachers.* Englewood Cliffs, NJ: Prentice-Hall, 1978.

Haines, Gail Kay. *The Elements.* New York: Franklin Watts, 1972.

Kent, Amanda, and Alan Ward. *Introduction to Physics.* Tulsa, OK: Usborne, 1983.

Lapp, Ralph E. *Matter.* Life Science Library. New York: Time-Life Books, 1963.

Ruchlis, Hy. *Bathtub Physics.* New York: Harcourt, Brace and World, 1967.

Silverberg, Robert. *Four Men Who Changed the Universe.* New York: G. P. Putnam's Sons, 1968.

Von Baeyer, Hans C. *Rainbows, Snowflakes and Quarks: Physics and the World Around Us.* New York: McGraw-Hill, 1984.

Westphal, Wilhelm H. *Physics Can Be Fun.* Alexandria, VA: Hawthorne Books, 1965.

Wilson, Mitchell. *Seesaws to Cosmic Rays: A First View of Physics.* New York: Lothrop, Lee and Shepard, 1967.

conservation of energy, law of: energy can neither be created nor destroyed. Also called *first law of thermodynamics.*

conservation of matter, law of: matter can neither be created nor destroyed. Also called *law of conservation of mass.*

definite proportions, law of: elements always combine in definite proportions by weight

energy: ability to do work. It can take the form of heat, light, electricity, mechanical energy, chemical energy, or nuclear energy.

Gay-Lussac's law: if pressure and temperature remain constant, equal volumes of gas contain equal numbers of gas particles. Also called *Avogadro's law.*

kinetic energy: energy of motion

mass: amount of matter an object or substance is made of

matter: any material—solid, liquid, or gas

Mendeleyev's periodic law: when arranged in order of atomic weight, the elements periodically repeat similar properties

multiple proportions, law of: atoms can combine with one another in different ways, but they still always combine in definite proportions

physics: the study of matter and energy and how they behave

scientific law: a statement that tells how things work in the universe

thermodynamics, second law of: in any energy transformation, some useful energy will be lost and turned into unrecoverable heat. Also called *law of entropy.*

valence: a combining number showing how an element joins with other elements

work: the amount of energy needed to move an object over a particular distance

atom, 17–26
atomic weight, 18, 23–27
Avogadro, Amedeo, 19, 52
Avogadro's law, 19

big bang, 48

caloric, 37
Carnot, Sadi, 45–46, 52
chemical reactions. *See*
    reactions, chemical
Clausius, Rudolf, 43, 52–53
compounds, chemical,
    15–22
conservation
    of energy, 35–41
    of mass, 10–11
    of mass and energy, 9
    of matter, 10–14

Dalton, John, 17–18, 23–24,
    53
    multiple proportions,
    law of, 18–19
definite proportions, law
    of, 17–18

Einstein, Albert, 8–9
elements, chemical, 16–33
    actinides, 31

alkali metals, 28
alkaline earth metals, 30
halogens, 30
inert gases, 31
rare earth elements, 31
energy. *See also* entropy,
    law of
heat, 37–47
kinetic, 35, 38, 40
law of conservation of
    (first law of
    thermodynamics),
    35–41
entropy, law of, 44–48

Gay-Lussac, Joseph-Louis,
    19–22, 53–54
Gay-Lussac's law, 19–21

heat death of the universe,
    47
Helmholtz, Hermann von,
    35, 54
Huygens, Christiaan, 35, 54

Joule, James Prescott, 35,
    37–40, 54–55

Kelvin, Lord. *See*
    Thomson, William

Lavoisier, Antoine-Laurent, 12–14, 55
law, periodic, 27–31
law, scientific, 6–9

mass, law of conservation of, 10–11
mass and energy, law of conservation of, 9
matter, conservation of, 10–14
Mendeleyev, Dmitri, 26–27, 30–31, 55–56
periodic law, 27–31
multiple proportions, law of, 18–19

natural law. *See* law, scientific
Newlands, John, 26, 56

periodic law. *See* law, periodic
periodic table, 27–33
Proust, Joseph-Louis, 17, 56
definite proportions, law of, 17–18

reactions, chemical, 16–17, 19–20, 23–24

Rumford, Count. *See* Thompson, Benjamin

scientific law. *See* law, scientific

table, periodic. *See* periodic table
thermodynamics. *See also* energy; entropy
first law of, 39–41
second law of, 42–48
Thompson, Benjamin (Count Rumford), 37, 57
Thomson, William (Lord Kelvin), 43, 57

universal law. *See* law, scientific

valence, 24–31

weight, atomic. *See* atomic weight

Index

About the Author

Paul Fleisher has written more than twenty books for young people and educators, including *Life Cycles of a Dozen Diverse Creatures*, the *Webs of Life* series, and *Brain Food*. His most recent books are *Gorillas* and *Ice Cream Treats: The Inside Scoop*. Paul is a regular contributor to *Technology and Learning* magazine. He has also created several pieces of educational software, including the award-winning *Perplexing Puzzles*.

Paul has taught in Programs for the Gifted in Richmond, Virginia, since 1978. He is also active in civic organizations that work for peace and social justice. In 1988, he received the Virginia Education Association's Award for Peace and International Relations, and in 1999 he was awarded the Thomas Jefferson Medal for Outstanding Contributions to Natural Science Education. In his spare time, you may find Paul walking through the woods, gardening, or fishing on the Chesapeake Bay. Paul and his wife of twenty-five years live in Richmond, Virginia.